To

_____

with all my heart!

one heart for two

An old proverb says that a man treating his wife like a princess is the best proof that he was raised by a queen. Even though today such terms tend to be considered as outdated, the truth is that we often raise our boys according to the image of the ideal man that we carry in our heads. And yet we, too, constitute a model for our sons on a very deep and subconscious level.

It may be the case that when they are five years old, they look at us straight in the eyes; and that when they are teenagers any show of tenderness can be a cause for war. By the time they are thirty-five, however, they suddenly realize that "there is no one else quite like mom."

From the moment they are born, we give them our hearts without a second thought. We do this to protect them from every adversity, and yet the time will come when we realize that the roles have now been reversed, and it is we who are now under their protection. This is a sacred, invaluable, ineffable fact, that no one should ever treat offhandedly.

My husband lost his mother several years ago. He often tells me how much he still wishes he could have had just one more moment with her. A chance to take her in his arms one more time, tell her that he continues to carry her in his heart. This is a book about everything that we would like to say to the most non-negotiable love of our lives, our sons.

To Vayitsa, for the love she gave to Costas so wholeheartedly, and for making him the man he is today...

Marina Gioti

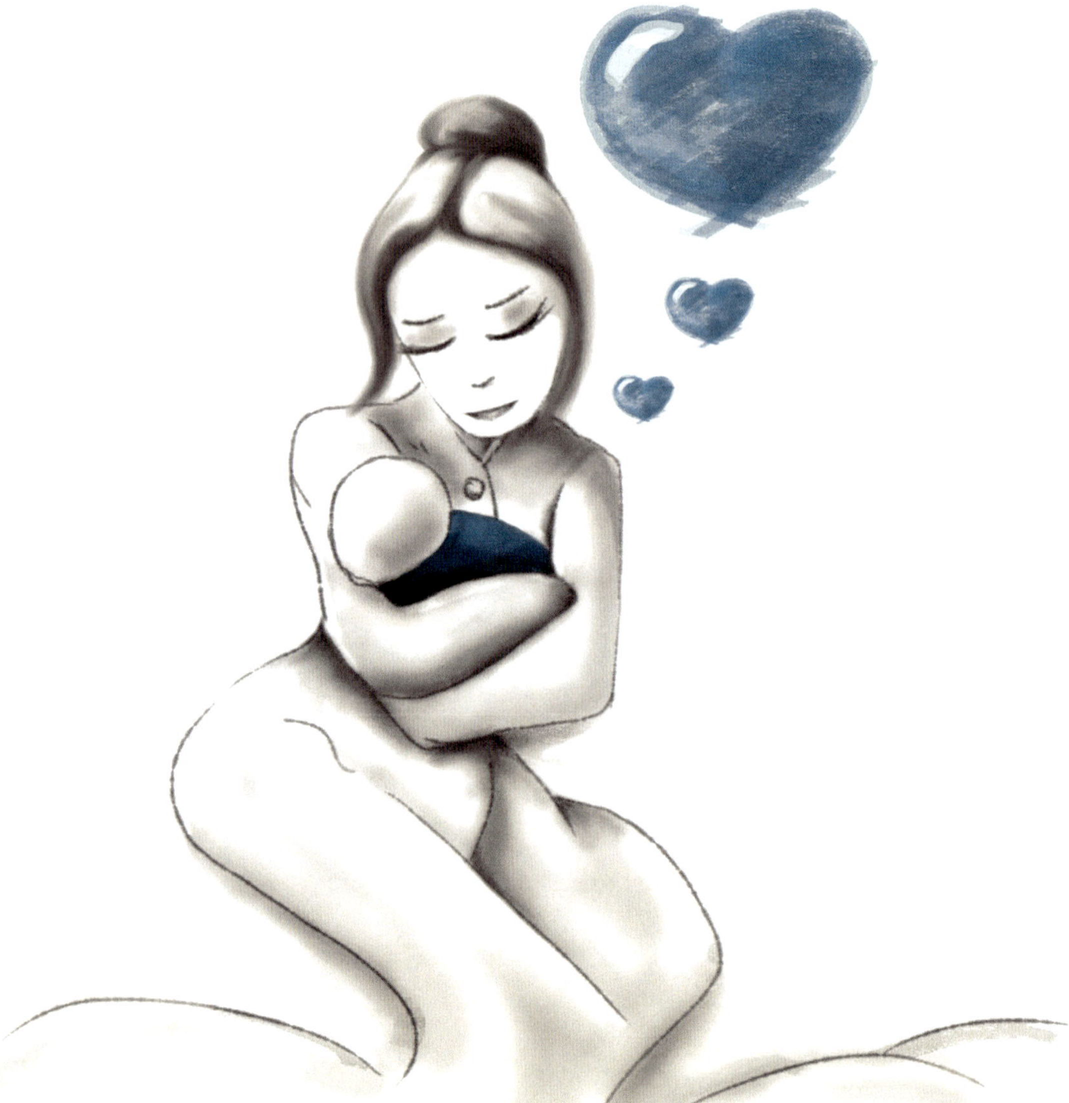

Darling,
my heart beat like

mad

the day you were born,
It did not take too long...

…for it to happen
– something no one had managed to do so far:
For you to steal my heart for ever, my little star,
so it would beat inside your chest from that day on,

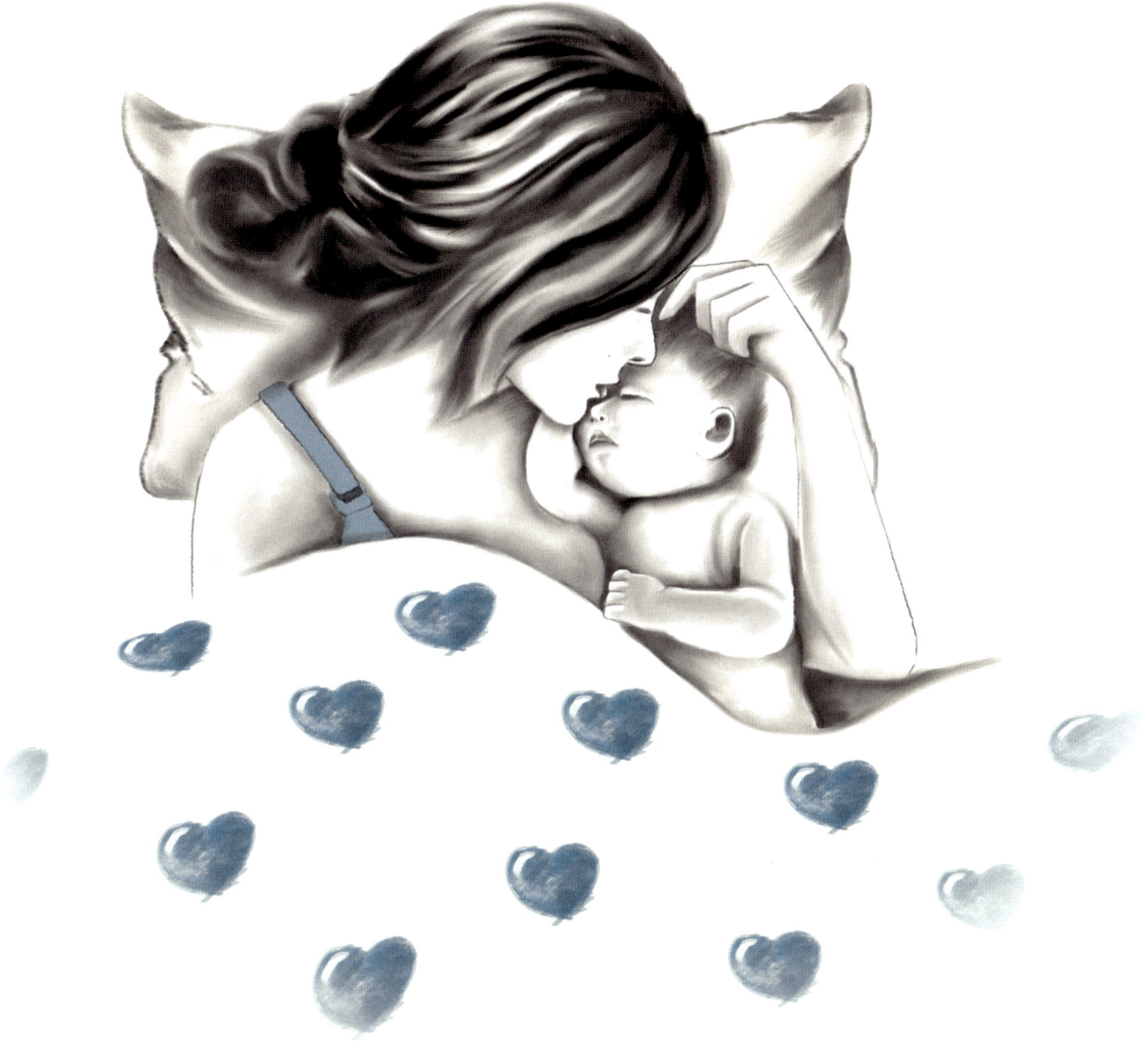

And it was

love

that took its place.
Innocent, like nothing I had known.
Spurring every sentiment with its infinity and grace.

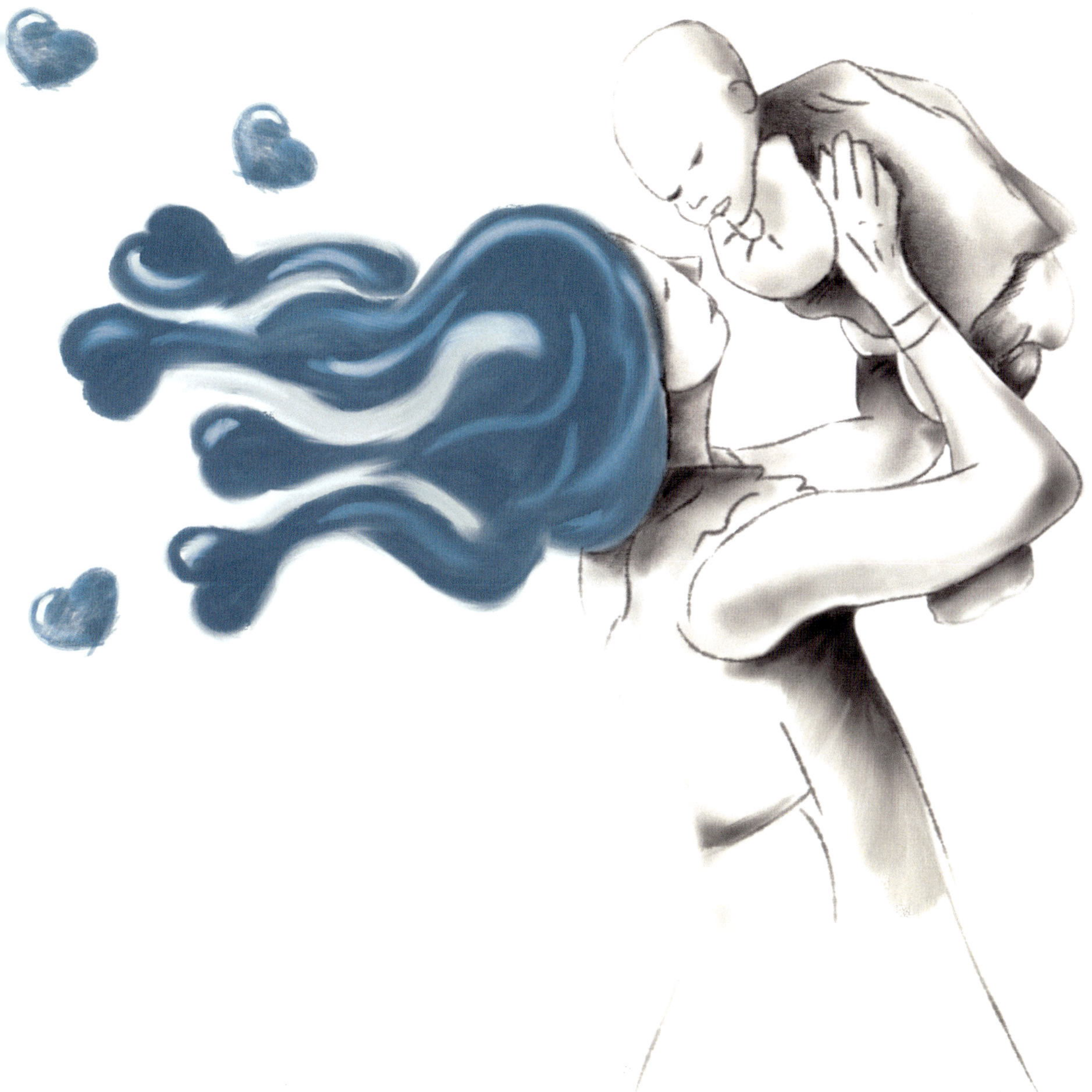

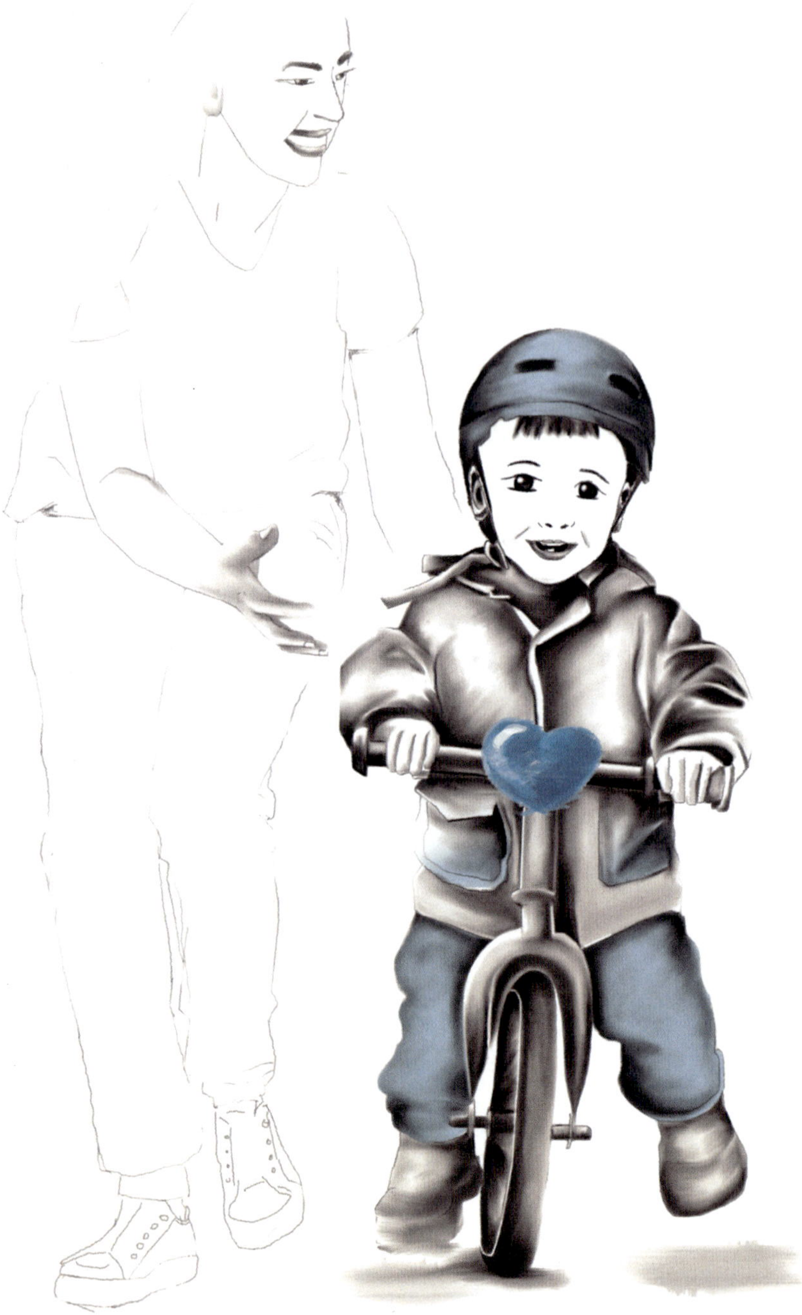

Your little heart now beats for two
from that day on, a single beat.
Therefore, my love, take double care. Once

for you

once also for me, my sweet.

For when you cry,
it is I who hurts and fills with tears.

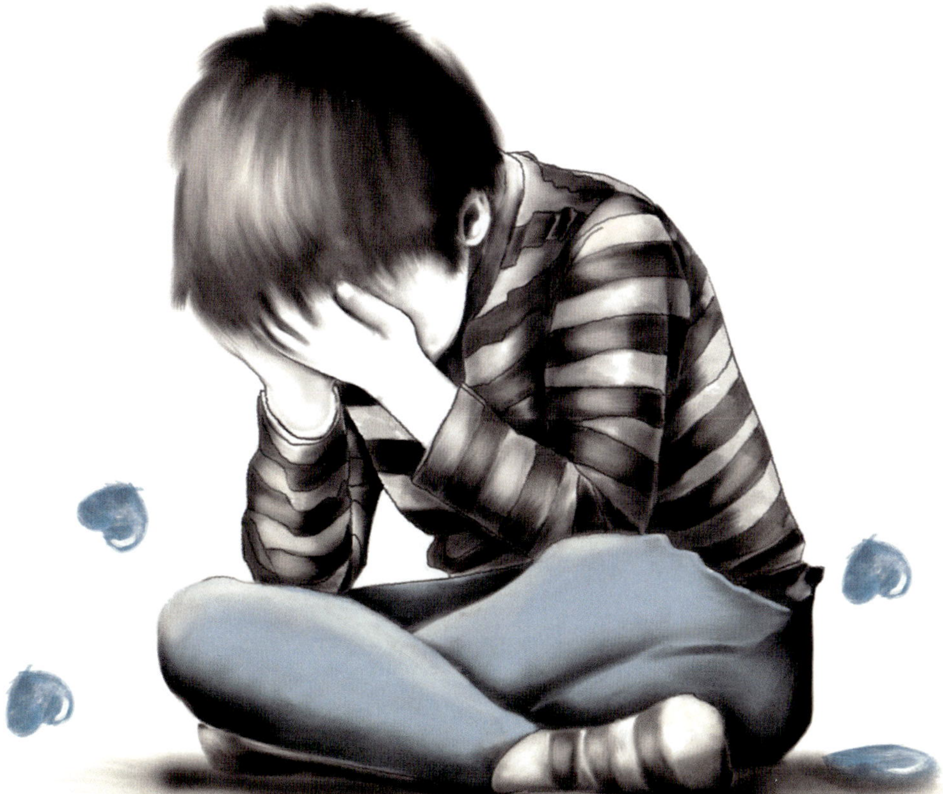

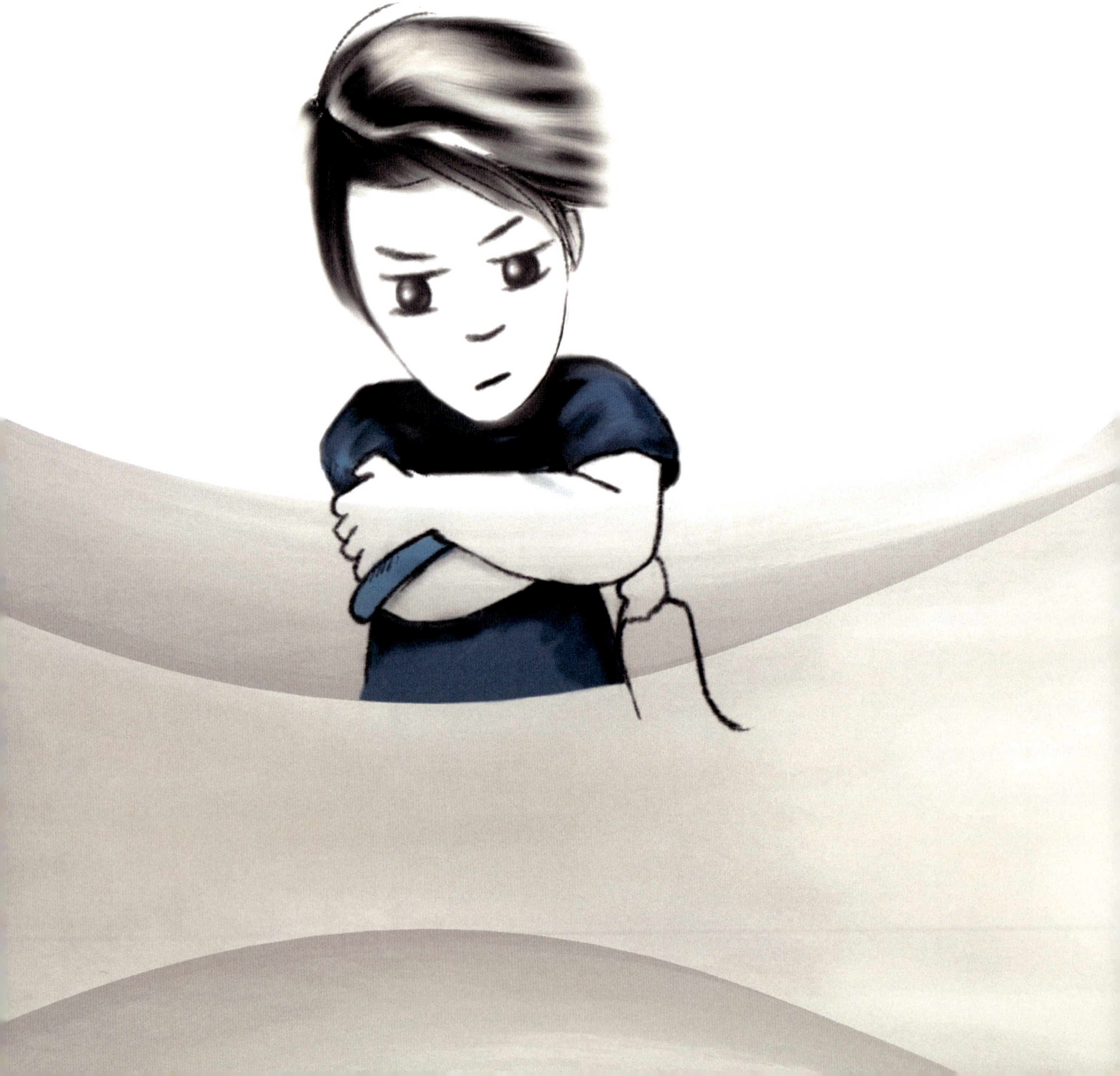

When you are cross,
storms rise inside me and I am broken,
pierced with spears.

You are disappointed,
and the world around us is painted grey,
is covered by a cloud.

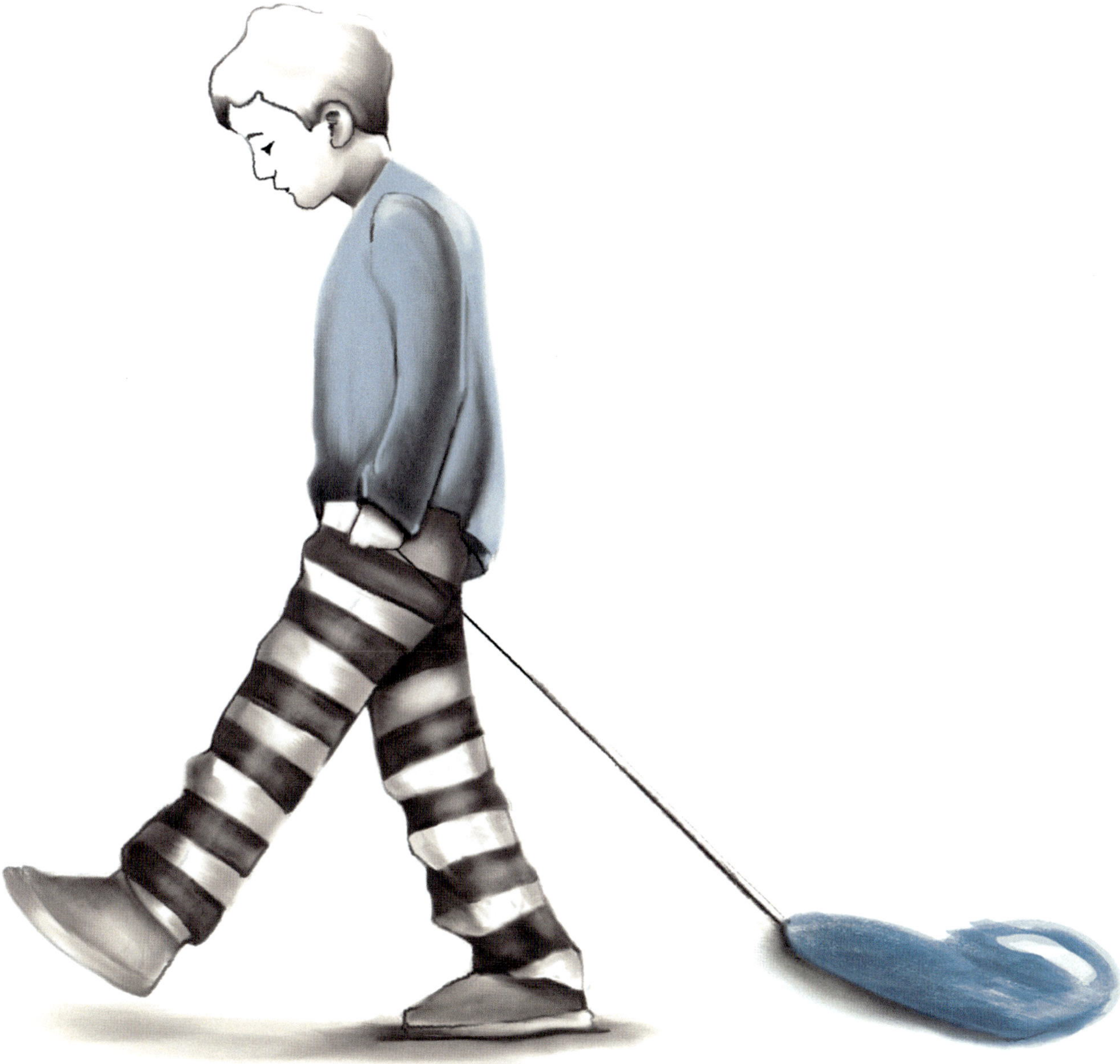

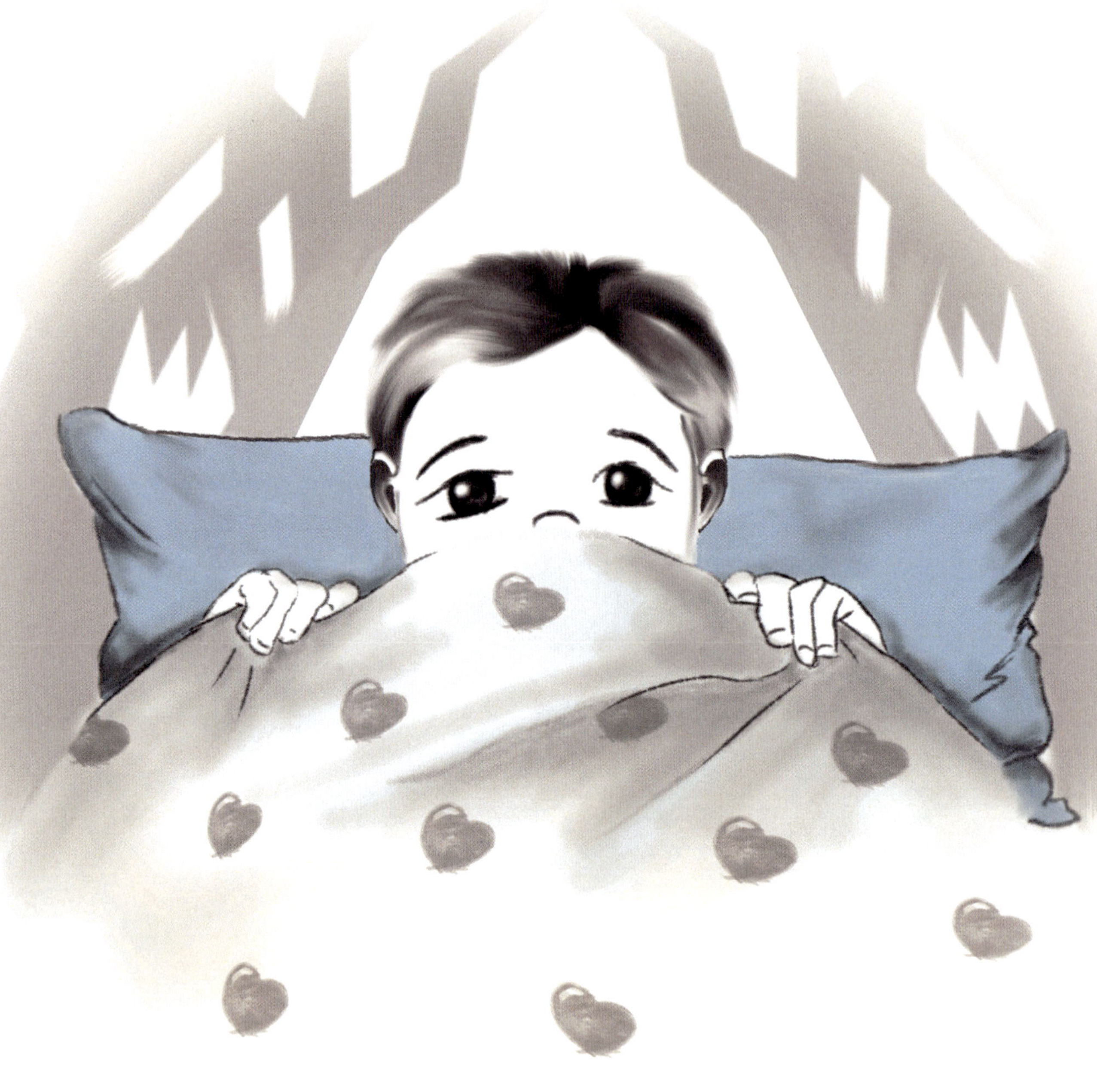

And when you are scared,
our one heart is crumpled,
like a paper shroud.

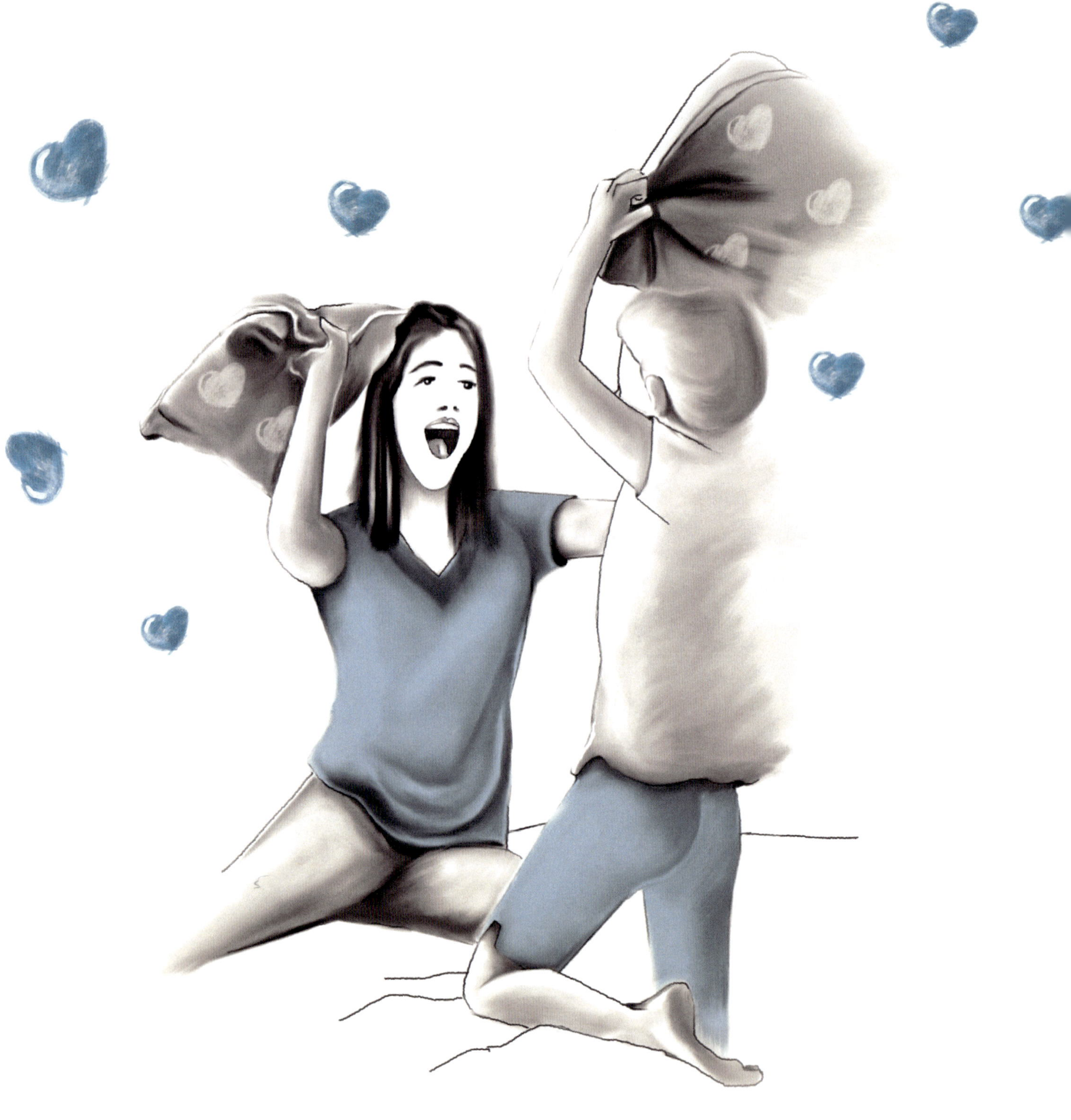

Yet when you laugh, I dance, amongst the fairest flowers, yearlong.

Your every dream
I make into wishes, and into song.

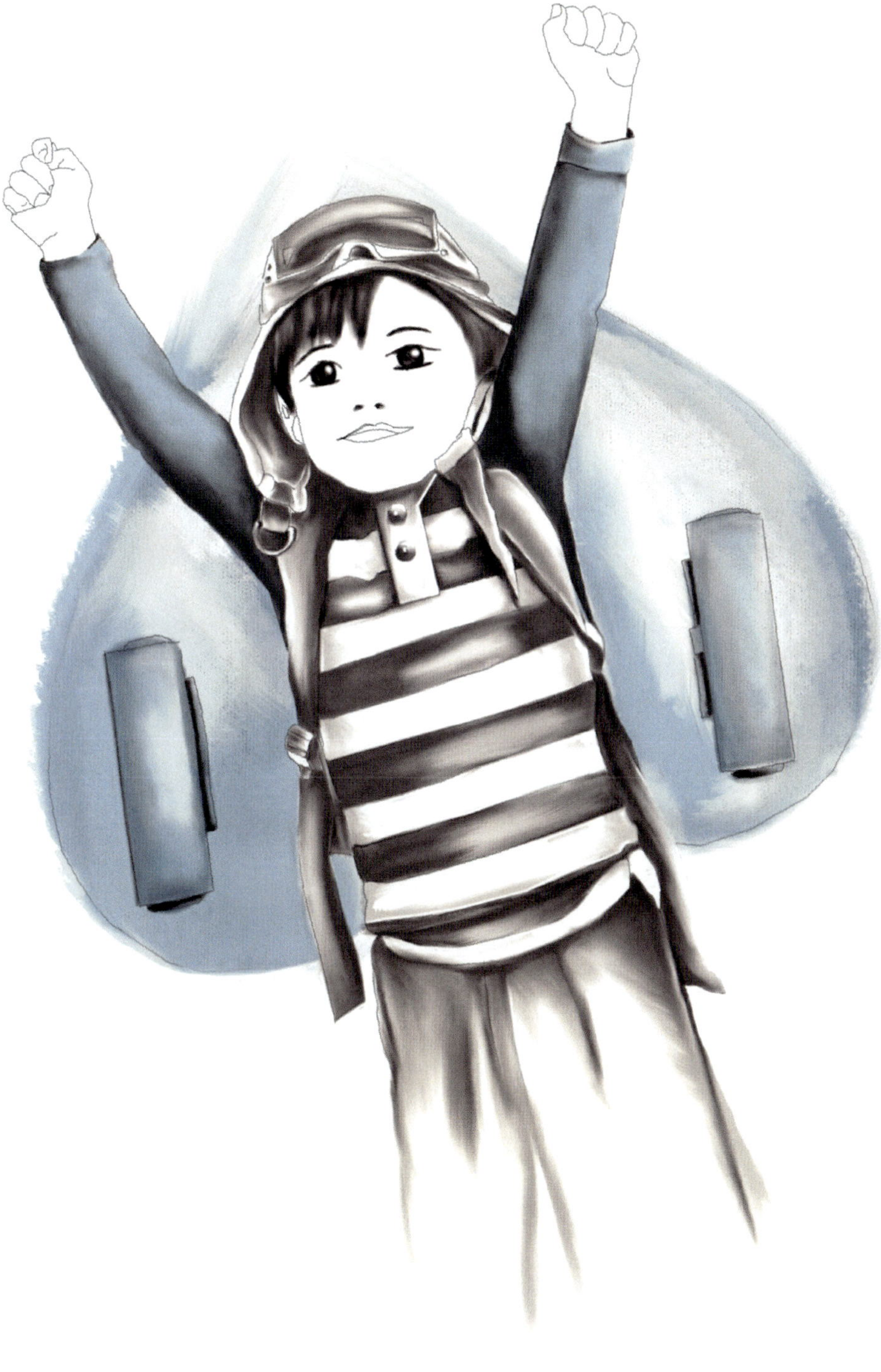

Your every breath becomes for me
a reason for a beautiful life.

Do not forget,

I shall always be there by your side.

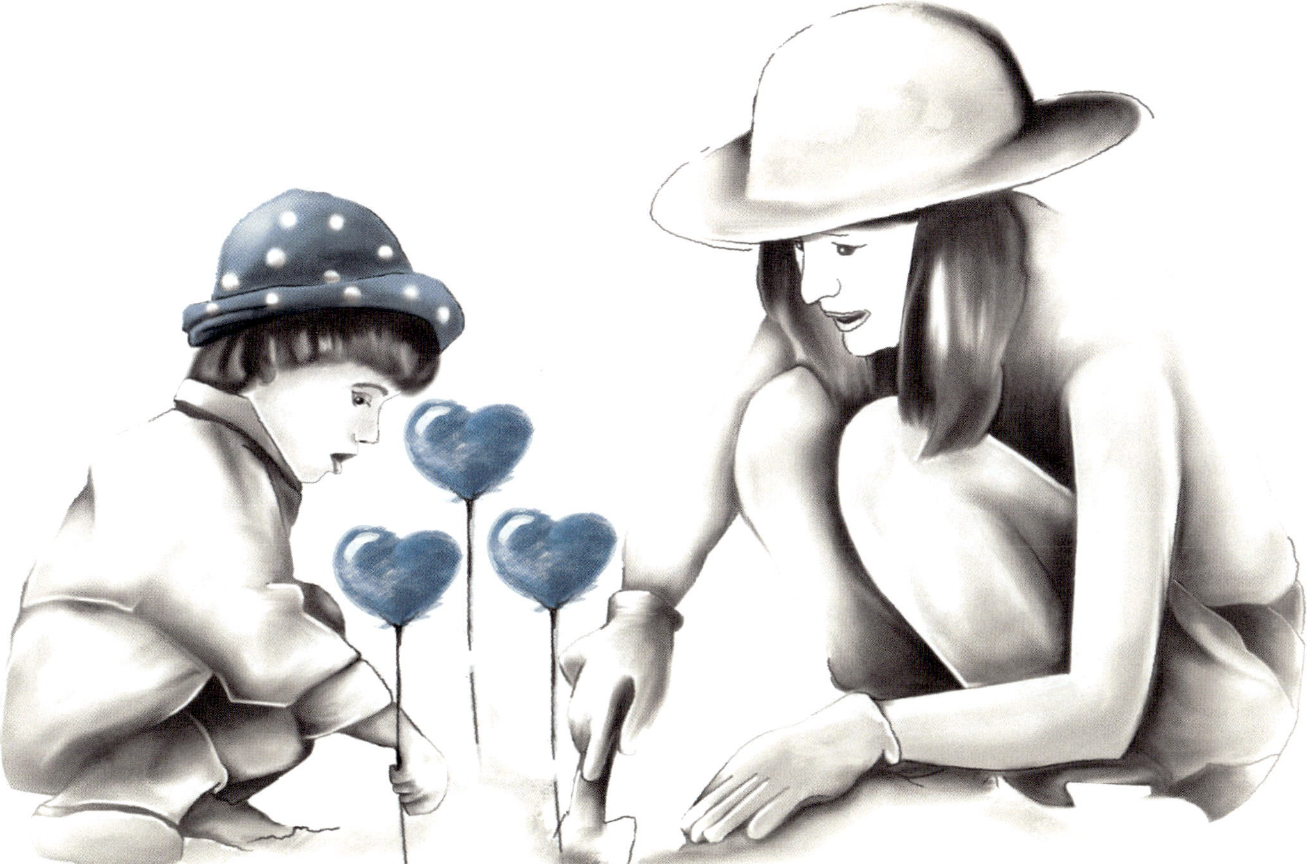

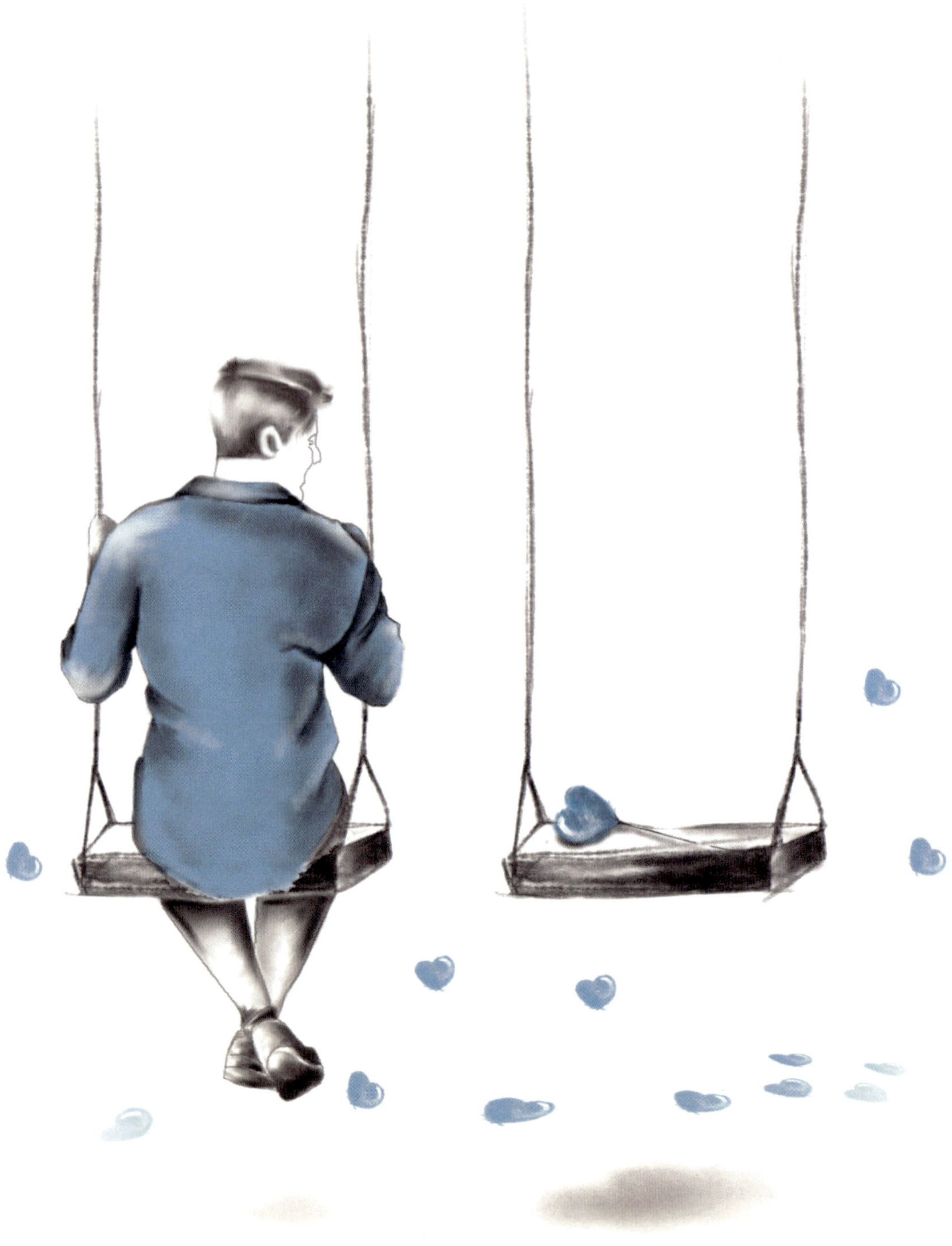

And when one day I will no longer be able
to be there with you,
know that I will always live
in your heart anew.

And when you struggle...

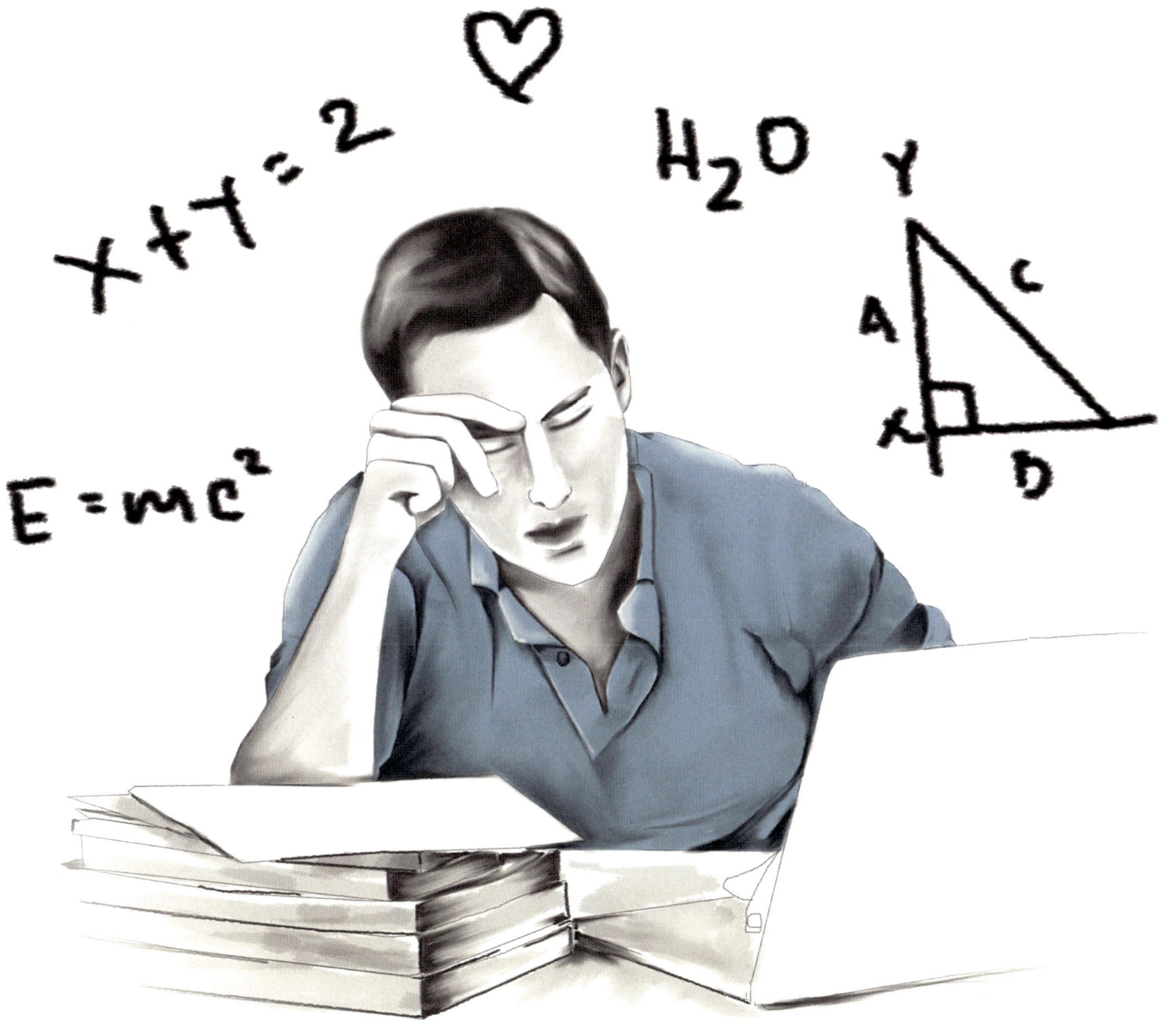
X+Y=2
H2O
Y
C
A
X
D
E=mc2

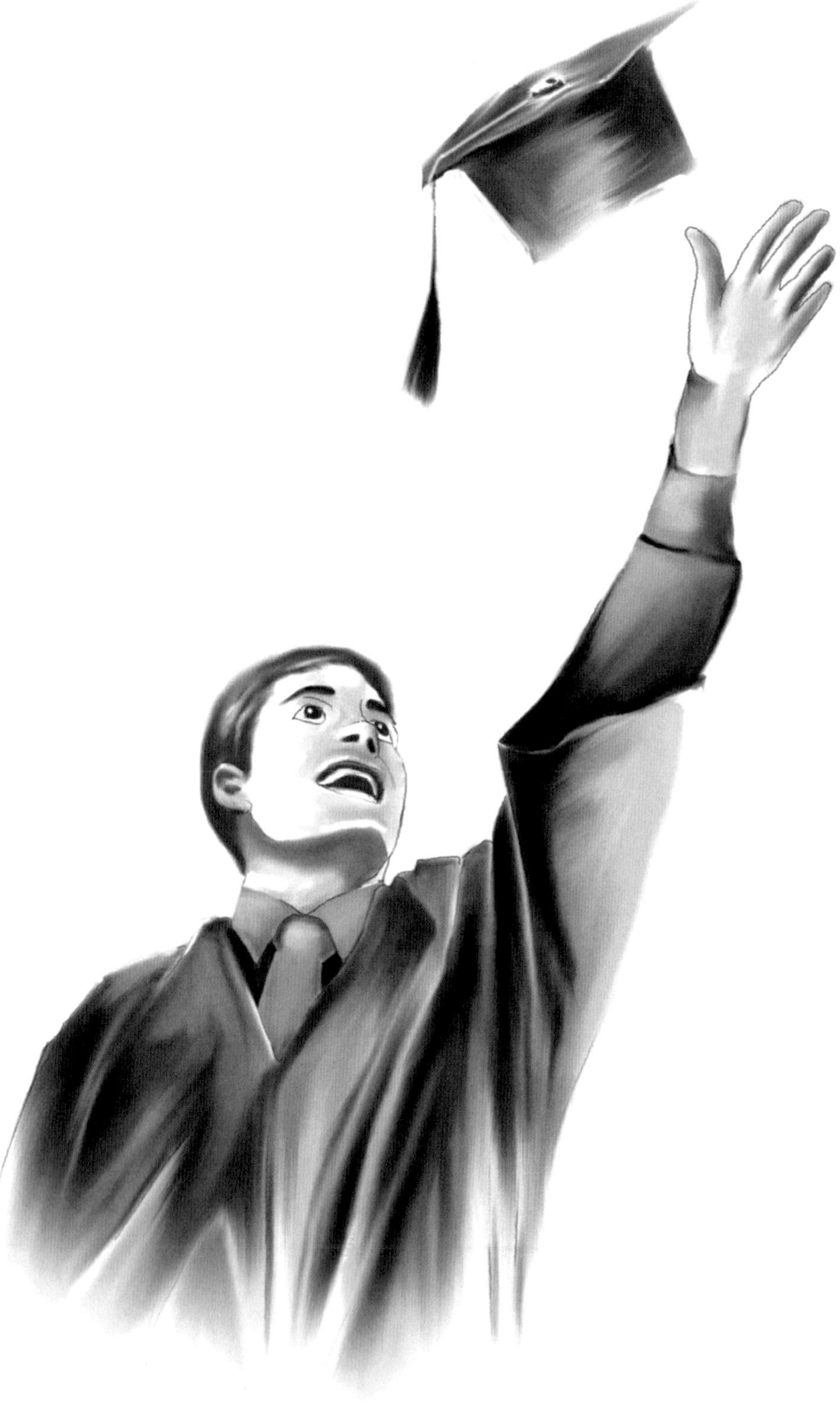

...and when you laugh...

...when you are scared
and in your fears you feel lost...

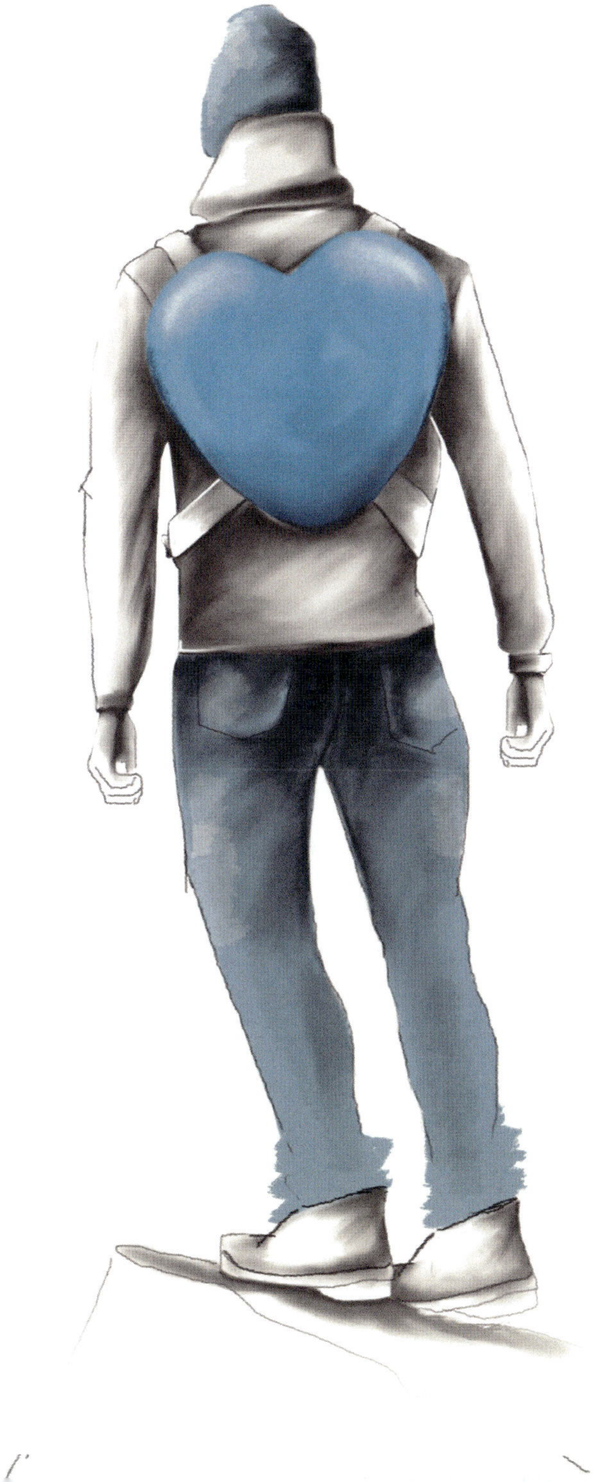

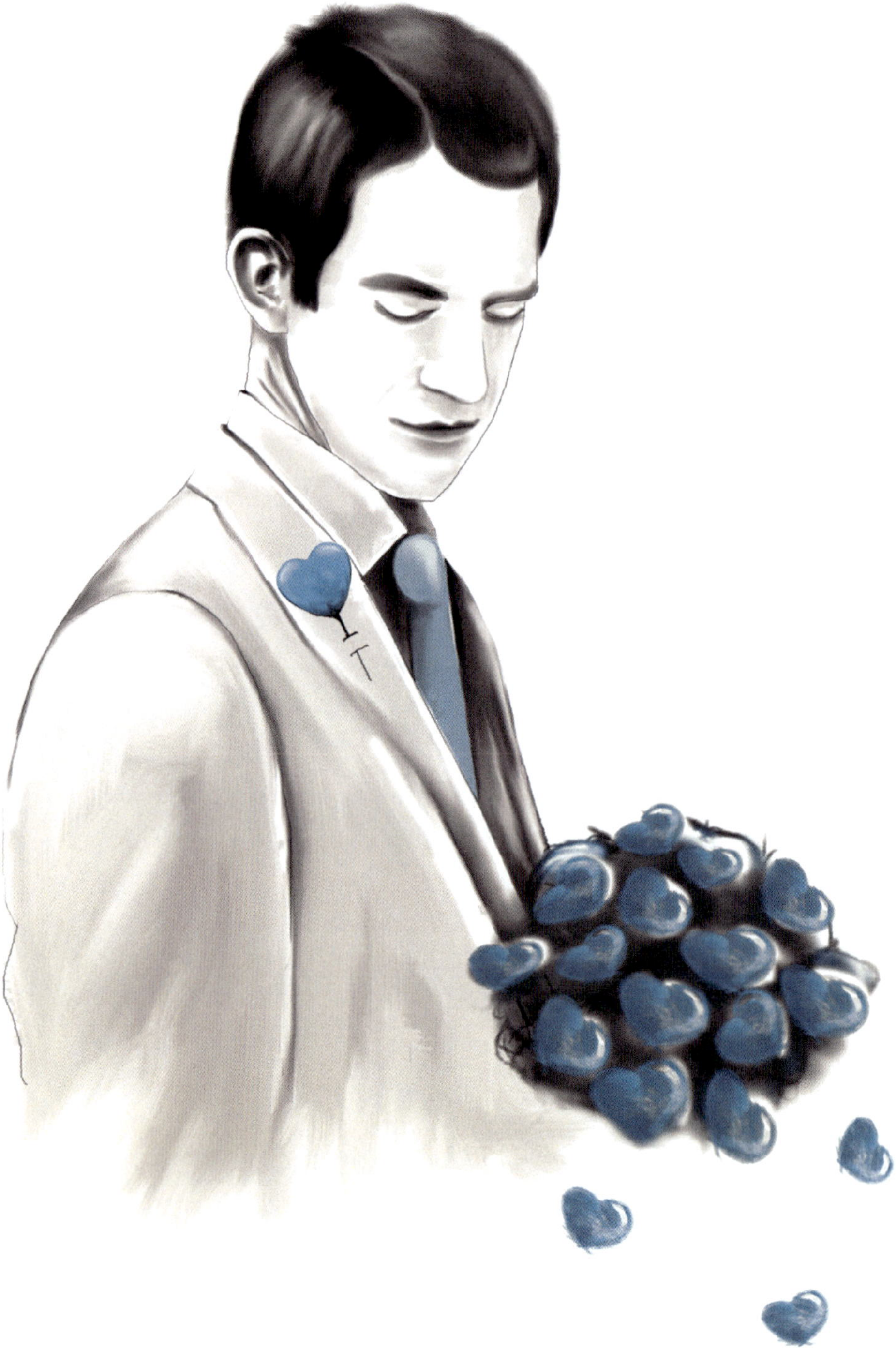

...I shall be there,
your faithful companion, at my post.
You shall feel me
with every beating of your heart.

Until that day comes
when you too will have to do your part.
To your own baby give yourself with all our heart.

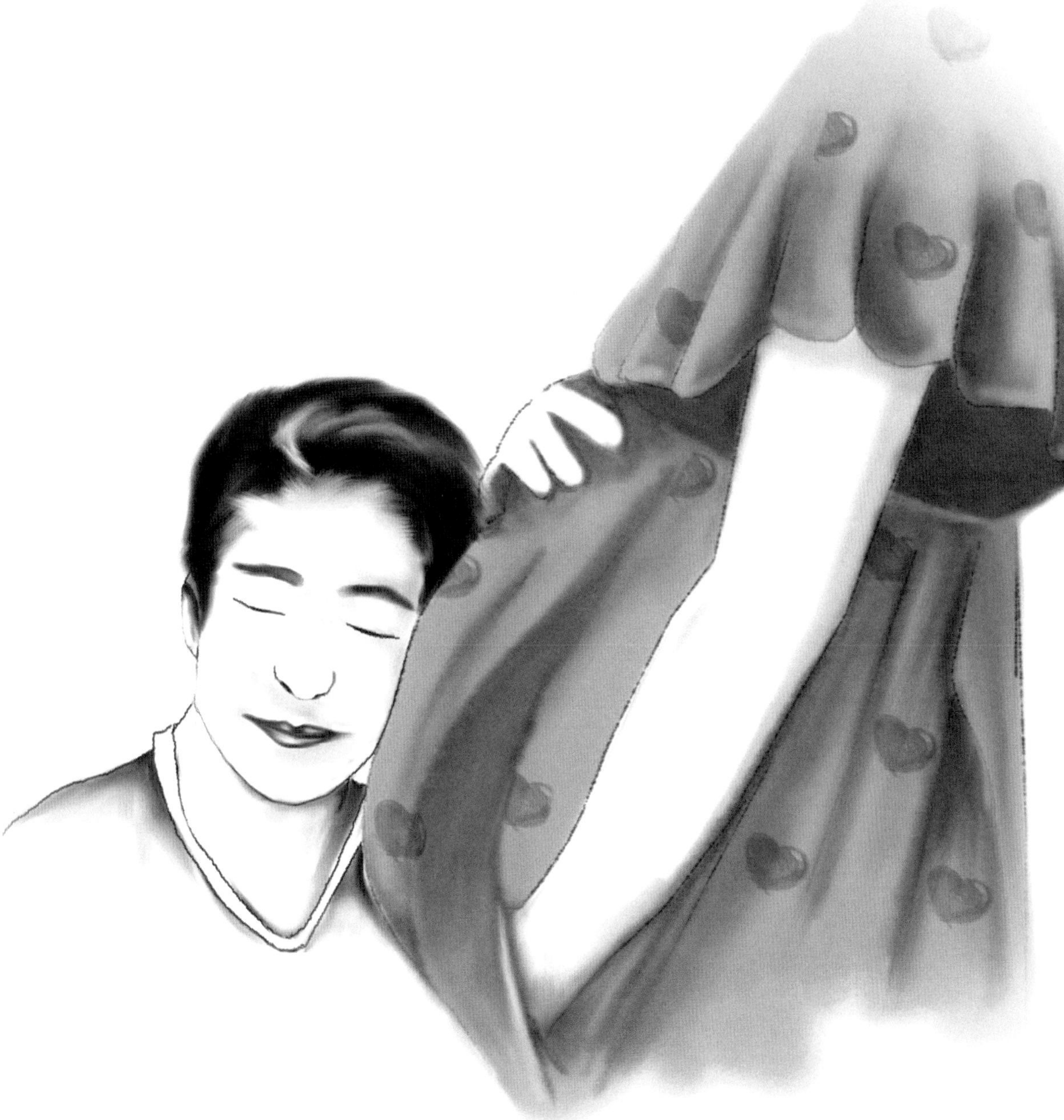

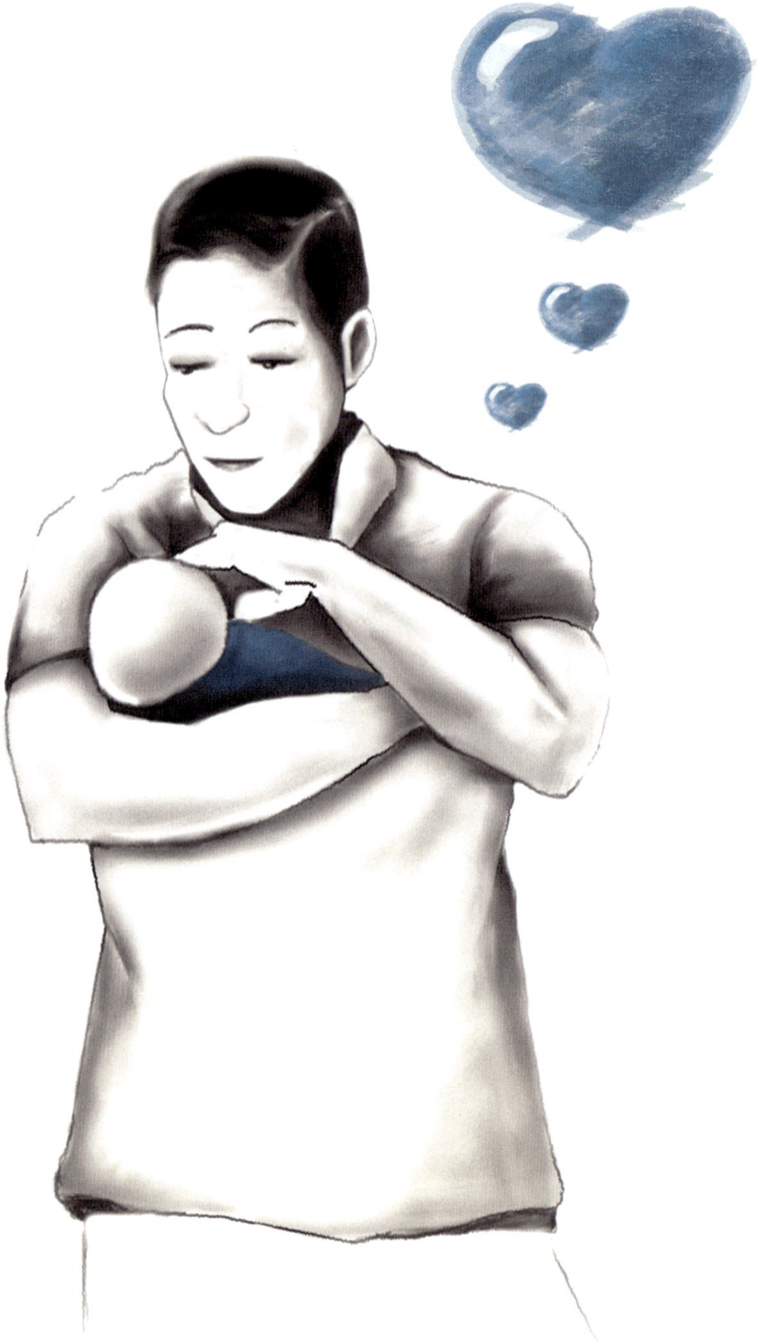

There too I will exist,
since there you will live.

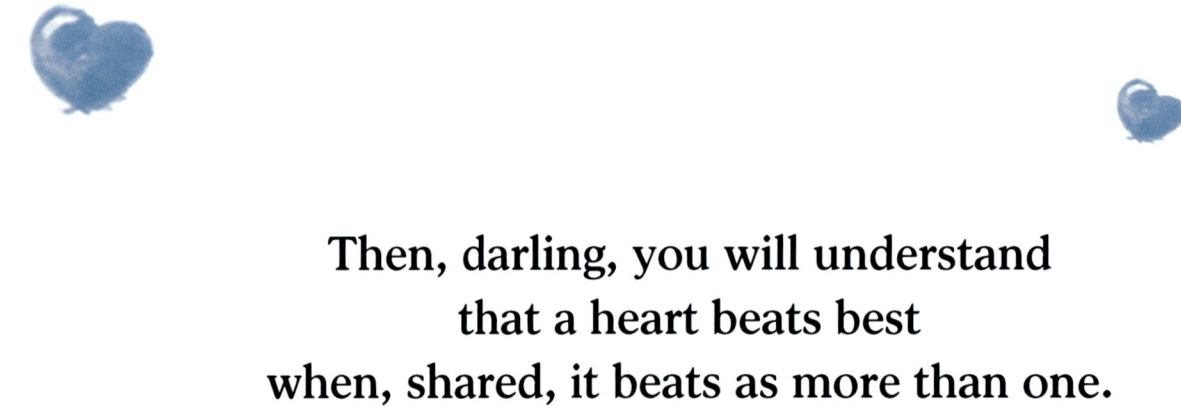

Then, darling, you will understand
that a heart beats best
when, shared, it beats as more than one.

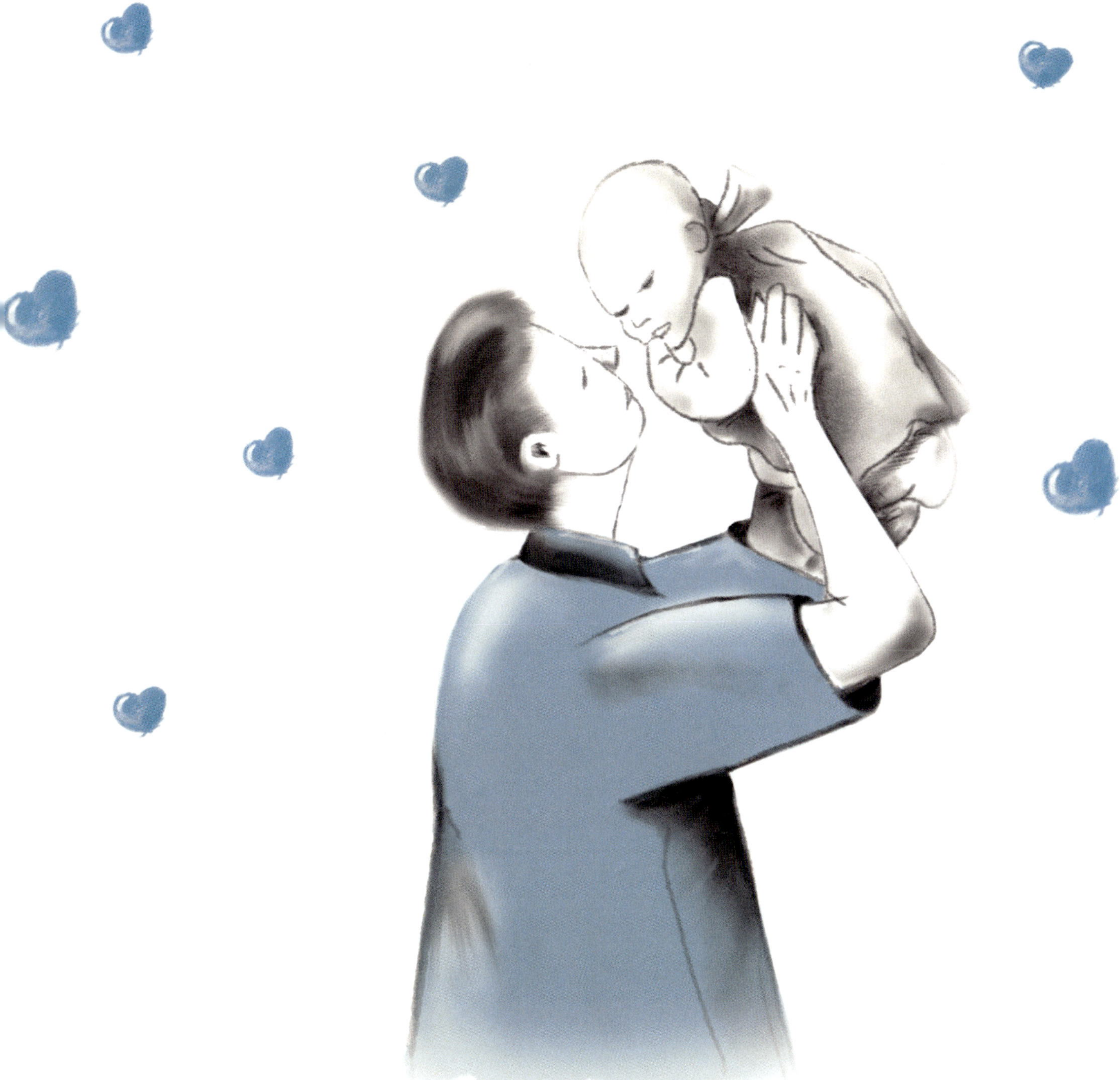

Marina Gioti Bio

Marina Gioti was born in Athens, Greece, in 1975. She studied Marketing and Fine Arts at Georgetown University in Washington, D.C., graduating in 1997. For the next two years she studied Visual Communication Design and illustration at the Pratt Institute in N.Y., graduating in 1999. She is a partner and the creative director at a visual communications company, and the chair of the Sunny Sports Club, a children's sports centre.

For her work in design, she has been the recipient of the John Peter's Publication Award and Scholarship from the Art Directors' Club in New York, as well as the International Pentaward.

Her first book, Momentita, was published in 2014, followed by Momentita is strong!, and the series Twice Upon a Time, Fairy tales retold, which so far includes the following titles: "Twice upon a time: Little Red Riding Hood" (listed among the 10 best picture books for 2016 by the Greek retailer Public); "Twice upon a time: Cinderella" and "Twice upon a time: Little Thumb" (voted by Public, Greece, among the 10 best picture books for 2017); and "Twice upon a time: What's Up with Santa Claus?", all published in Greece by Dioptra Publications. Her first book for mothers and daughters, with the title One Heart, was published in 2017 and has been an instant success. Translated into two languages, it reached No1 in its category on Amazon.

Her books, originally written in Greek, have been translated into English and Italian. She is the mother of a ten-year-old daughter.

Amazon author page: amazon.com/author/marinagioti

© J.D. Strikis

You can contact Marina:

- marina@marinagioti.gr
- Marina Gioti
- MarinaGioti
- marina_gioti
- Marina Gioti

www.marinagioti.gr

Written and Illustrated by
© Marina Gioti, 2019. All Rights Reserved

First Edition in Greek, March 2019

Translated into English by Mika Provata-Carlone

Thank you for taking the time to read 'One Heart for two'! If you enjoyed it, please tell your friends or post a short review on Amazon or Goodreads. Word of mouth is an author's best friend and much appreciated!

Find out more about Marina and her books at
www.marinagioti.gr